SBB

SWASTICK BOOK BOX
MASON OF WINNERS

English
WRITING BOOK
Capital Letters

Awesome English Writing Practice Book for Kids

By: **Preeti Garg**

Follow the patterns with your pencil.

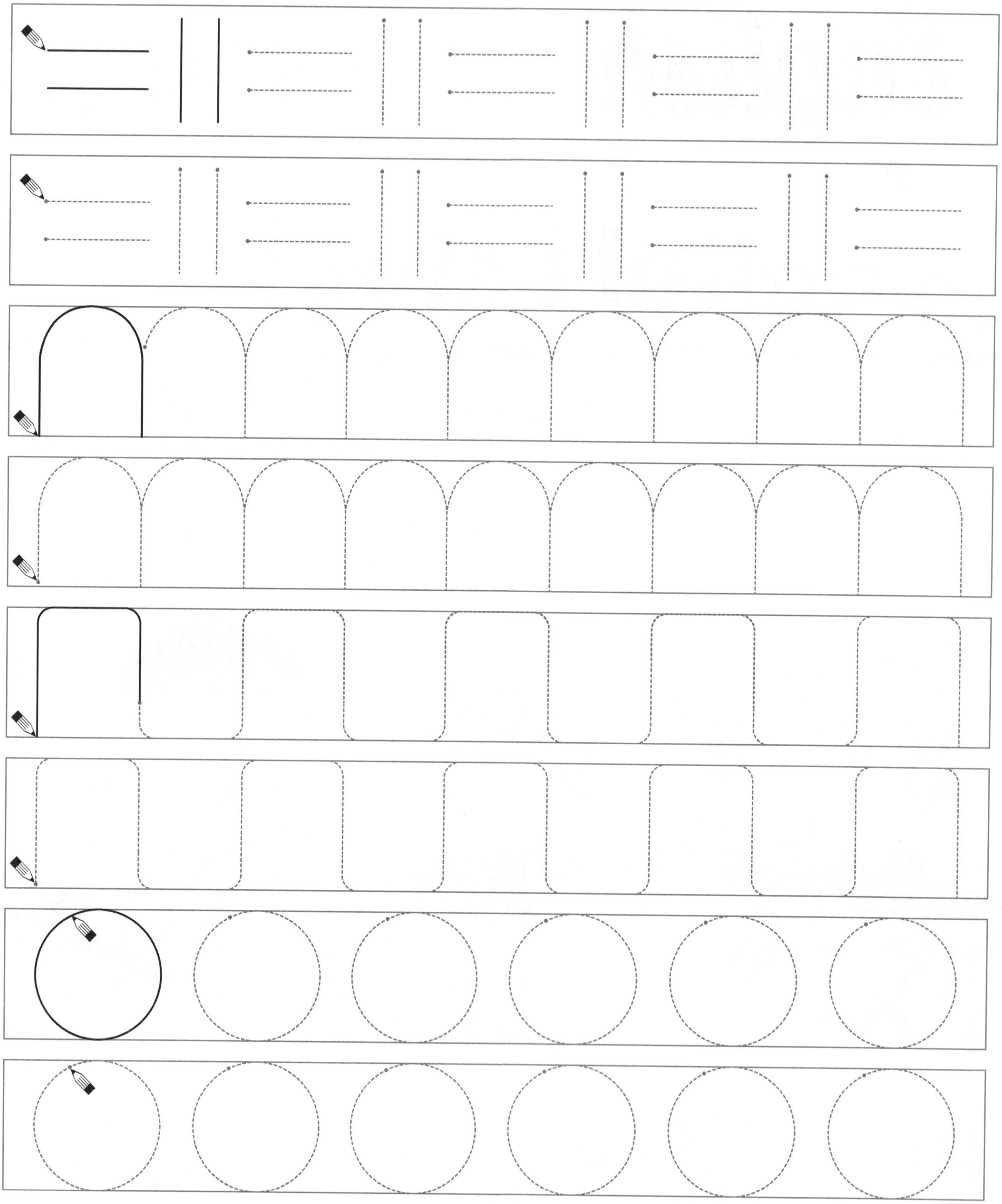

Date : ....

Teacher's Signature : ....

Follow the patterns with your pencil.

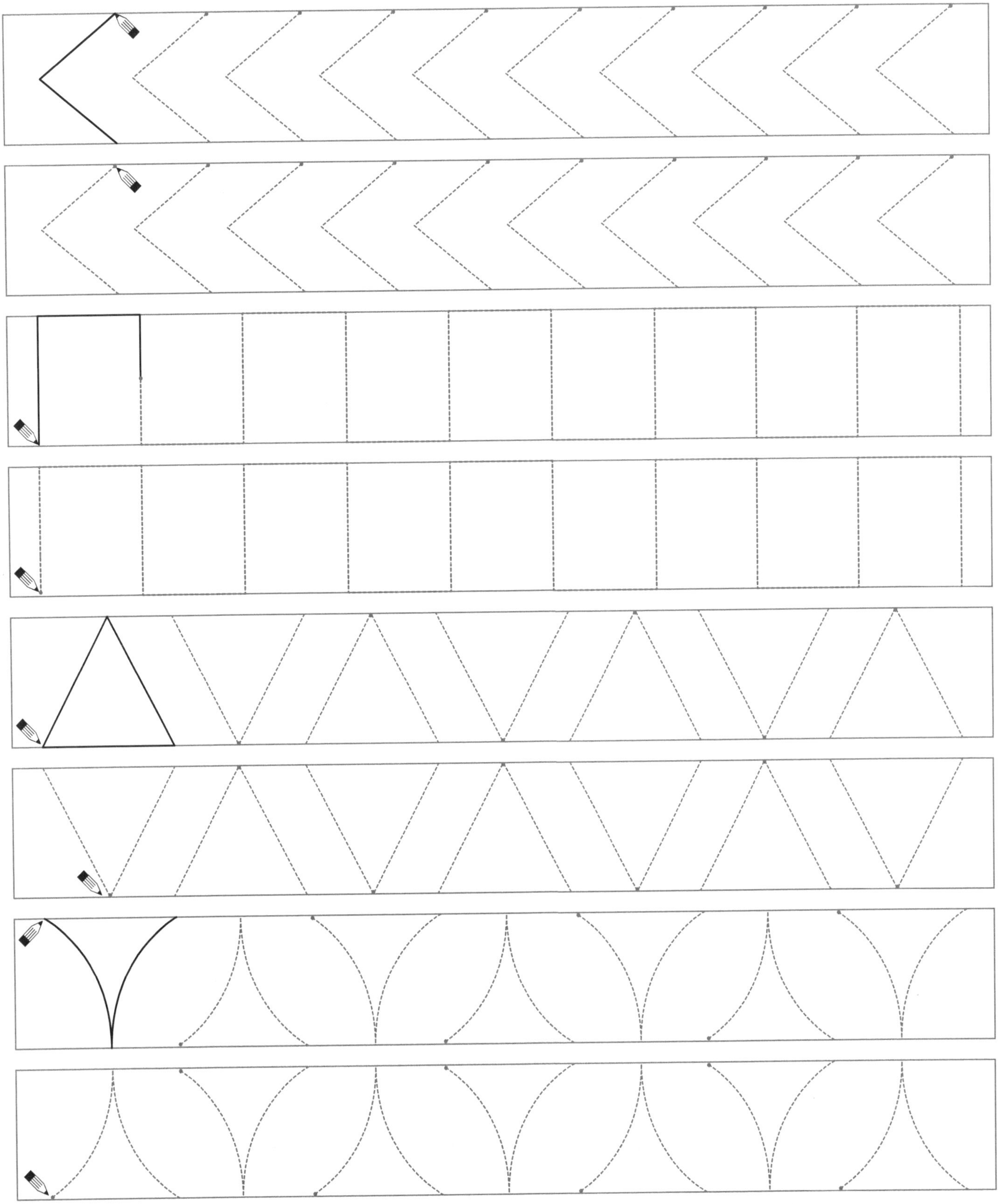

Date : ....

Teacher's Signature : ....

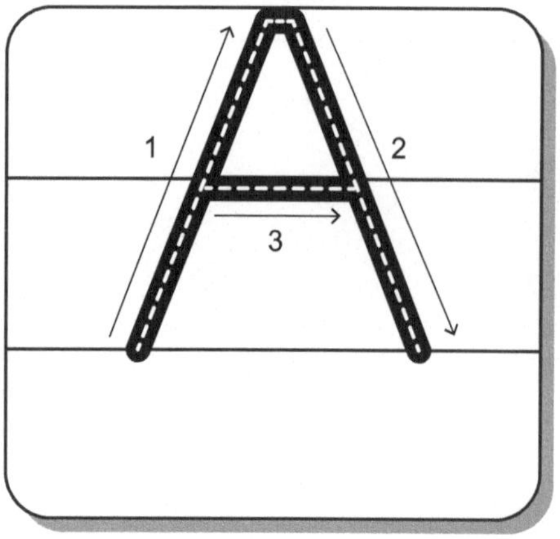

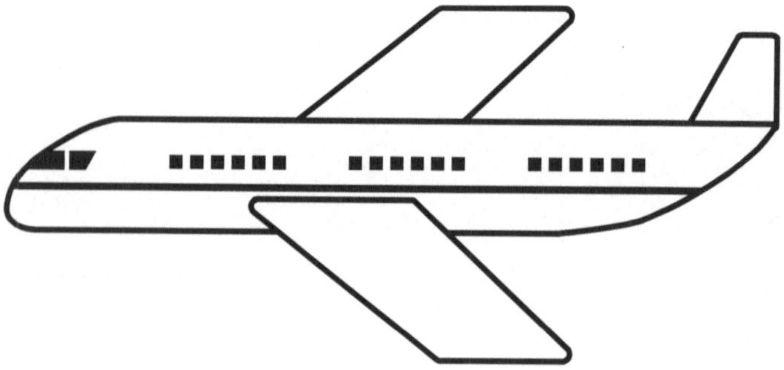

Aeroplane

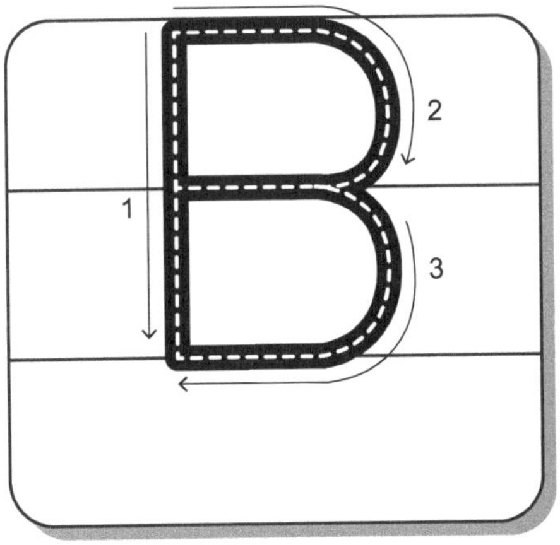

Banana

Date : ....

Teacher's Signature : ....

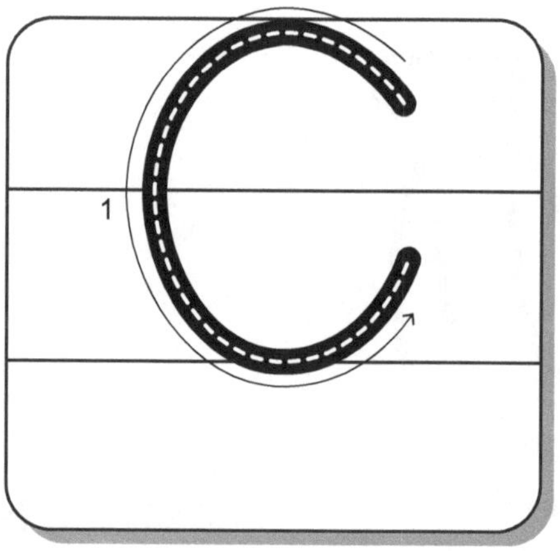

Cake

Date : .... Teacher's Signature : ....

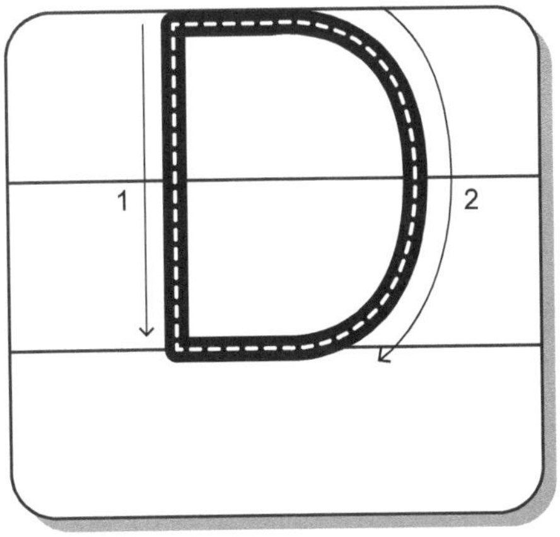

Dog

D

Date : ....

Teacher's Signature : ....

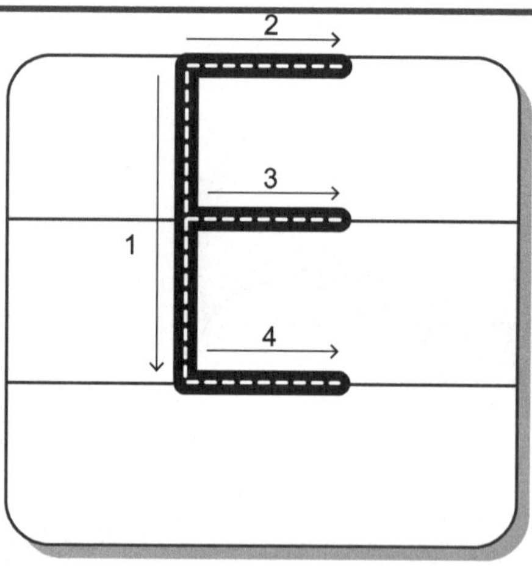

Engine

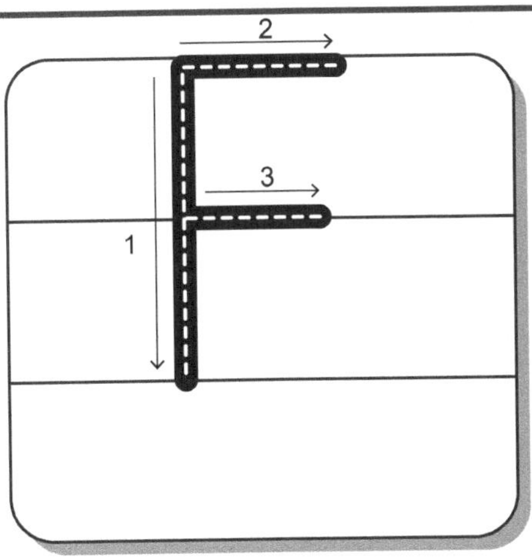

Flower

F

Date : ....

Teacher's Signature : ....

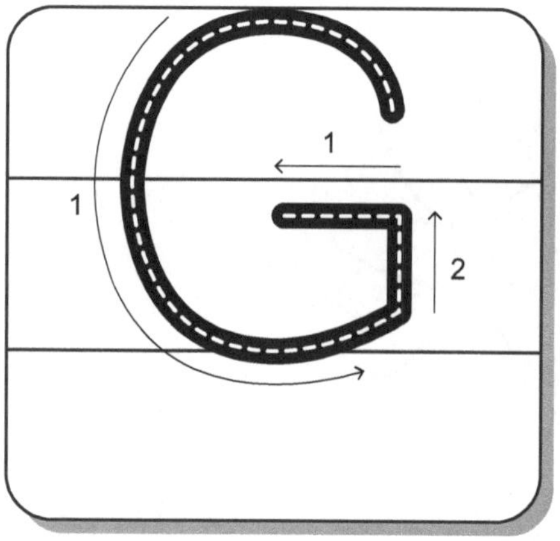

Girl

Date : ....

Teacher's Signature : ....

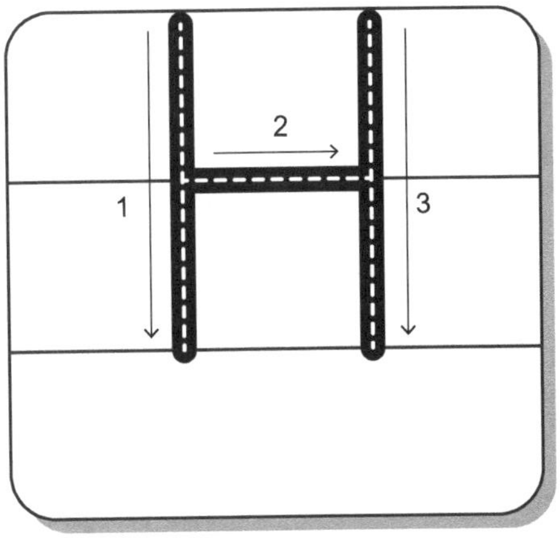

Hen

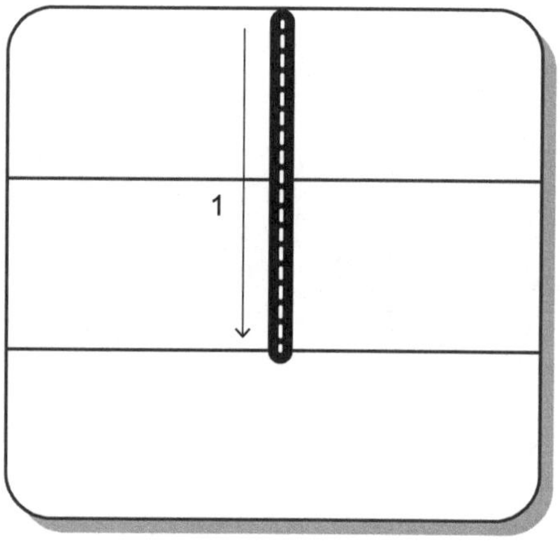

Inkpot

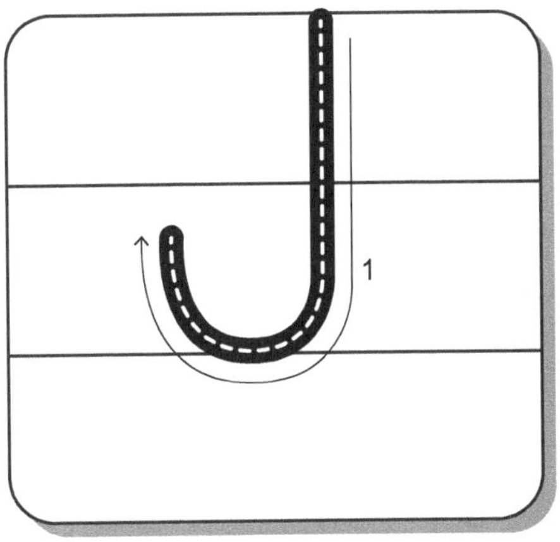

Jug

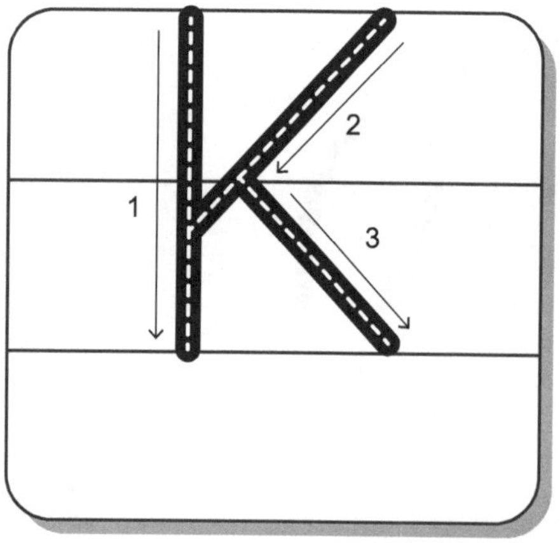

King

K

Date : ....

Teacher's Signature : ....

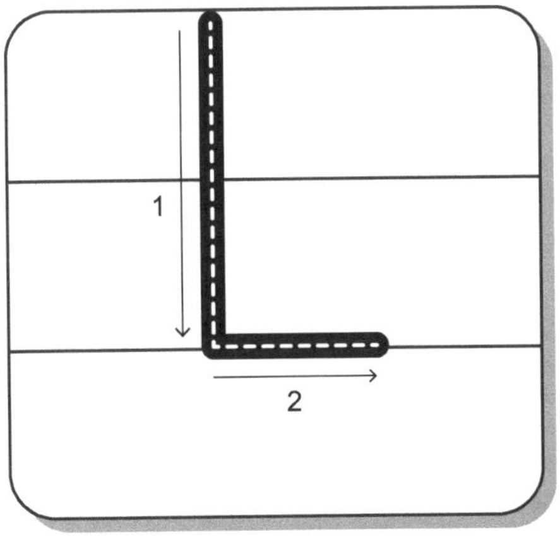

Lamp

Date : ....

Teacher's Signature : ....

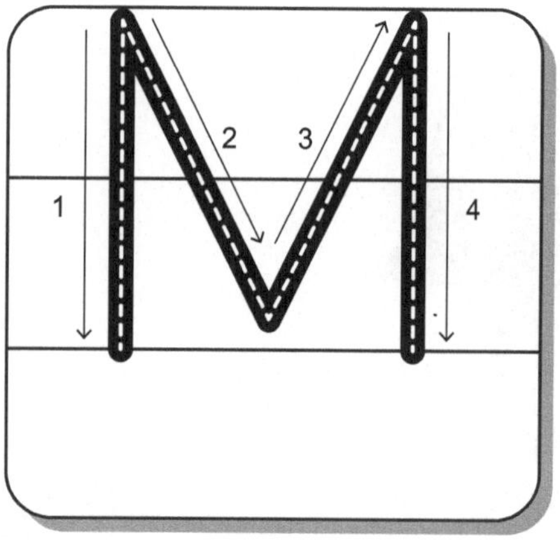

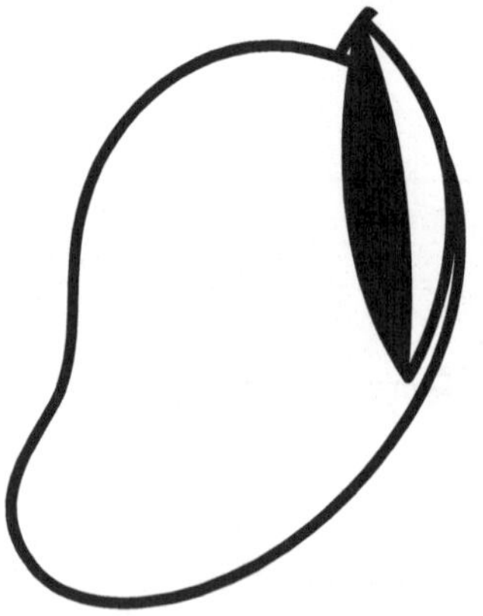

Mango

M

Date : ....

Teacher's Signature : ....

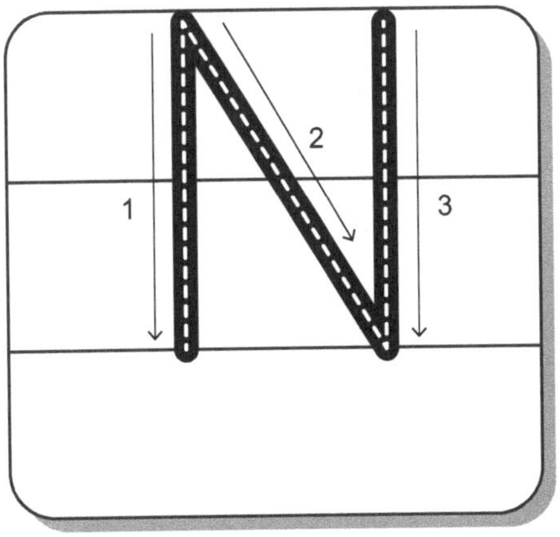

Nest

N

Date : ....

Teacher's Signature : ....

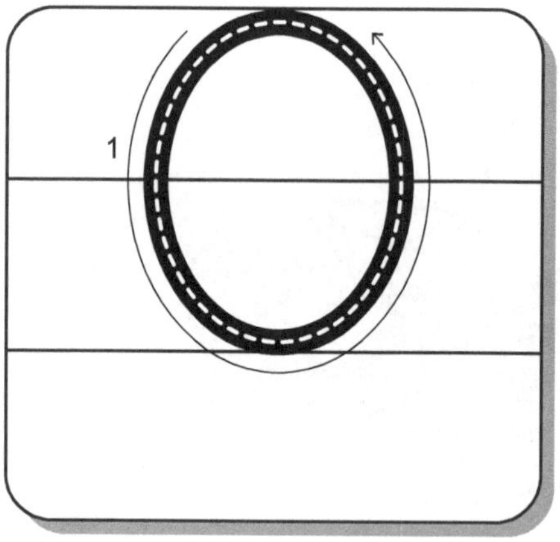

Octopus

Date : ....

Teacher's Signature : ....

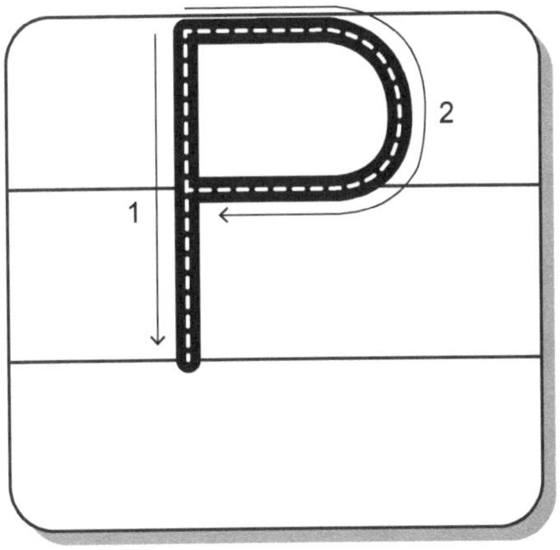

Parrot

P

Date : ....

Teacher's Signature : ....

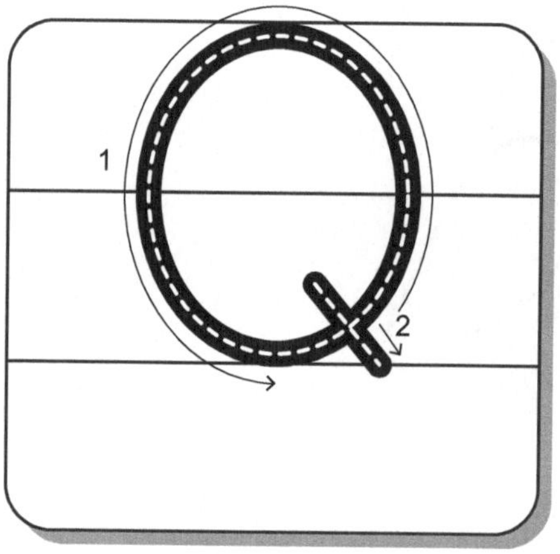

Quilt

Q

Date : ....

Teacher's Signature : ....

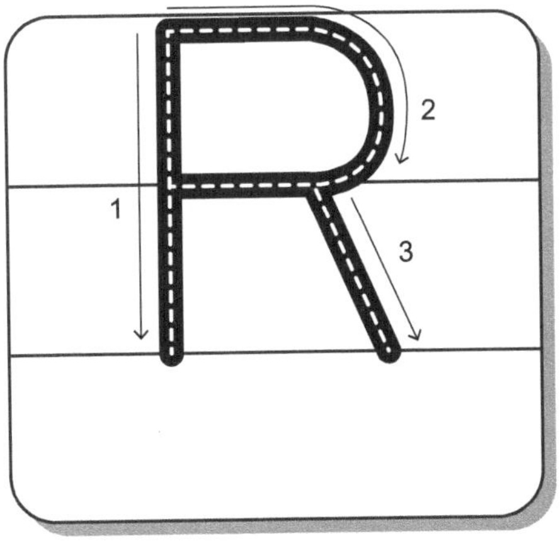

Rainbow

Date : ....

Teacher's Signature : ....

Snowman

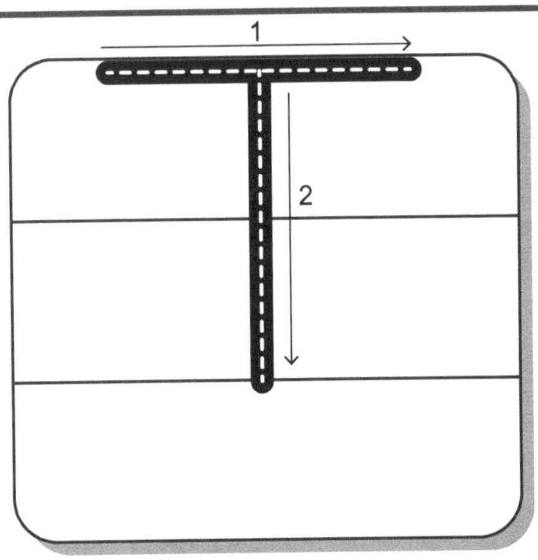

Train

Date : ....

Teacher's Signature : ....

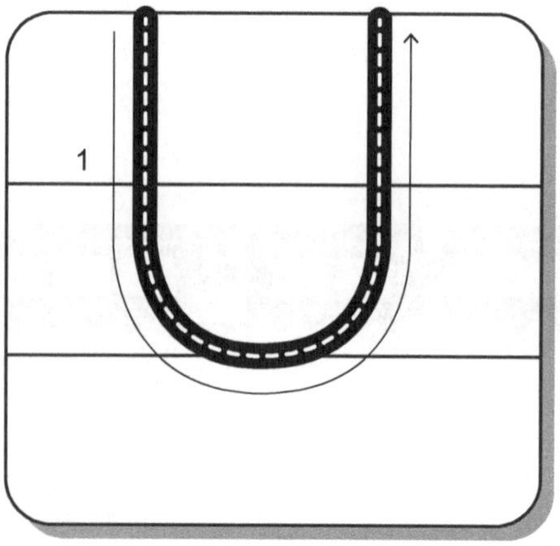

Umbrella

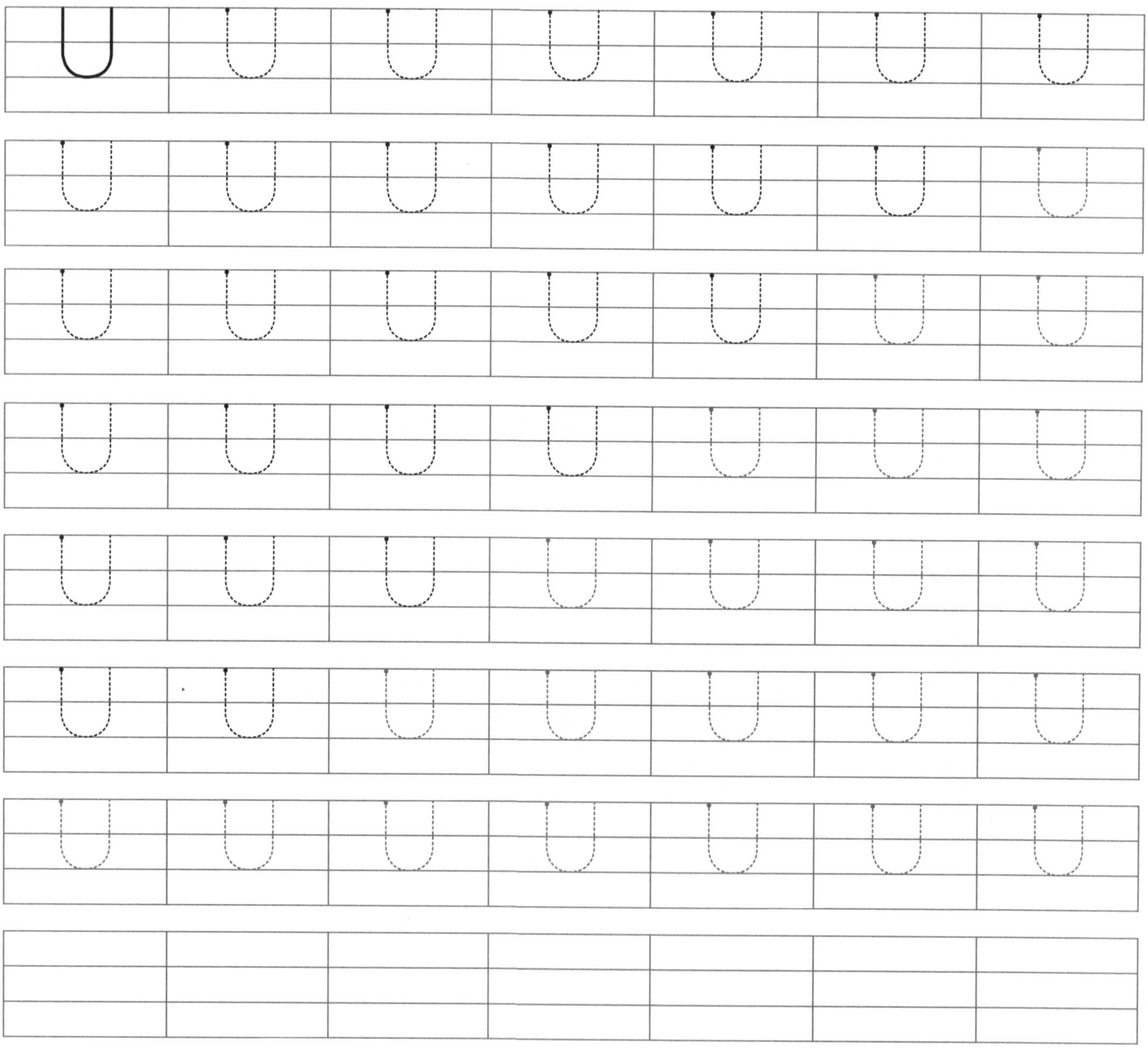

Date : ....

Teacher's Signature : ....

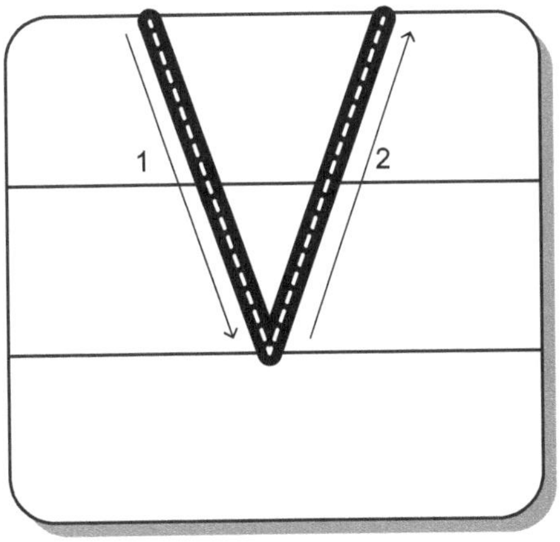

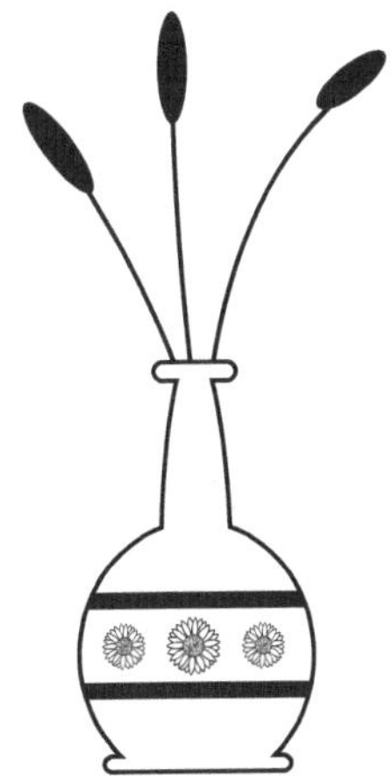

Vase

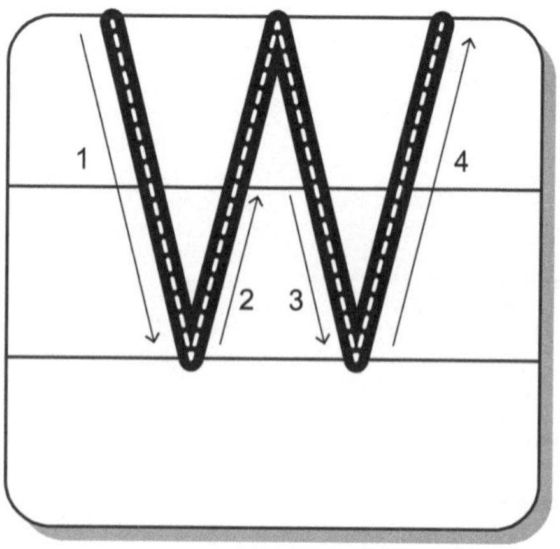

Watermelon

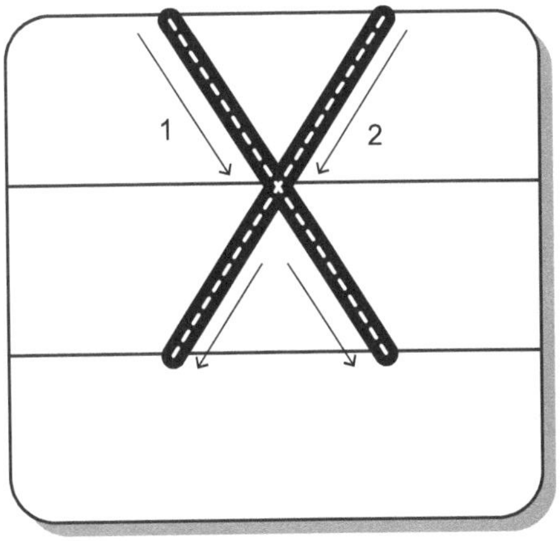

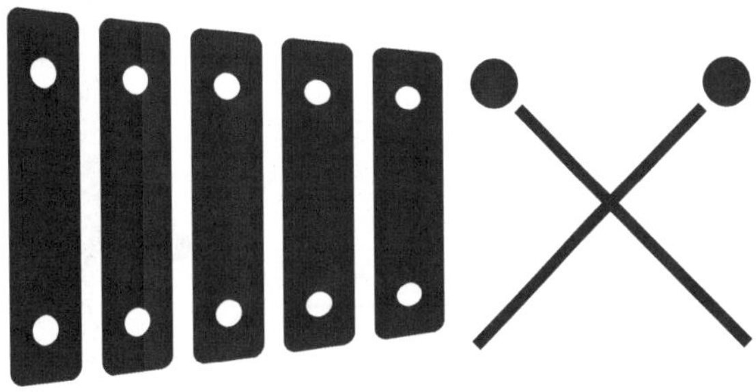

Xylophone

Date : ....

Teacher's Signature : ....

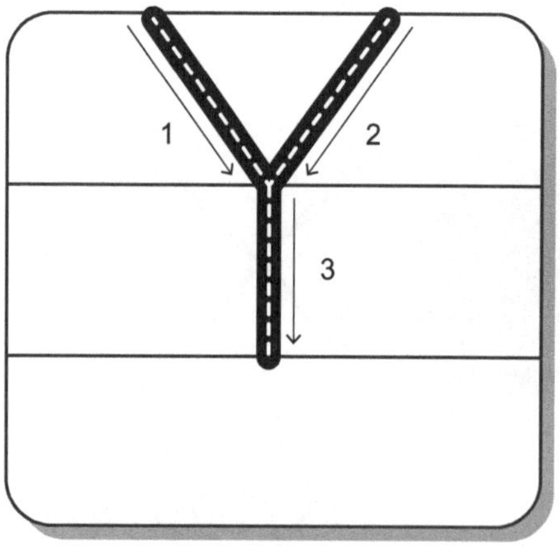

Yoga

Date : ....   Teacher's Signature : ....

1
2
3
Zoo

Say and trace the letters.

A	B	C	D	E	F
G	H	I	J	K	L
M	N	O	P	Q	R
S	T	U	V	W	X
Y	Z				

Write the letters A to Z.

Date : ....

Teacher's Signature : ....

Write the missing letters from A to Z.

A	B		D	E	
G	H	I			L
M				Q	R
	T	U	V		
Y	Z				

Write the letter that comes after the given letter.

U		P		O	
C		L		Q	

Write the letter that comes before the given letter.

	N		Y		K
	V		H		I

Date : ....

Teacher's Signature : ....

Match and write the letters with objects they start with.

F

R

B

W

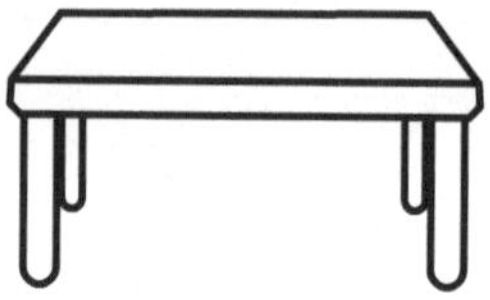

J

L

T

P

Date : ....

Teacher's Signature : ....